# EMOTIONS IN GOD'S WORLD

written by
**Beverly Beckmann**

illustrated by
**Jules Edler**

CONCORDIA®
Publishing House
St. Louis

In God's world we all smile, laugh, wink,

**hug, kiss, cry.**

**Sometimes we are afraid.**
**It's alright to be afraid.**

**Even Jesus' followers were afraid when the wind and the storm**

**caused their boat to fill with water.**

**But Jesus stopped the storm and told His followers, "You don't have to be afraid." Jesus helps us, too.**

**Sometimes people hurt our feelings.**
**It's alright to feel hurt.**

**Even Jesus' feelings were hurt when people called Him names.**
**But Jesus forgave those people.**
**Jesus helps us forgive others, too.**

**Sometimes we get angry.**
**It’s alright to be angry sometimes.**

Even Jesus was angry at the money changers in the temple.
But His anger went away after a while.
Jesus helps our anger go away, too.

**Sometimes we feel we want to be alone.**
**It's alright to feel that way.**

**Even Jesus wanted to be alone after feeding 5,000 people.**

**Then, when Jesus was alone, He prayed to God the Father.**

**Jesus helps us pray, too.**

**Sometimes we feel very sad, and we cry.**
**It's alright to feel sad and to cry.**

**Even Jesus cried when His friend Lazarus died. But Jesus knew that people who believe in Him will live in heaven because God loves them. Jesus helps our sadness go away, too, when He tells us that He loves us.**

**However we feel, God is with us.**
**And when we are not happy, God wants to help us.**
**He even asks us to ask in prayer for His help.**

Dear Family Members,

God has given us the gift of emotions. As adults, we know what they are. We know when we are angry or happy, and we say so.

But children do not know how to verbalize their emotions. Many times they will simply say, "I'm tired," because they don't understand, "I'm upset." This verbalization will develop as they grow older.

In the meantime, we can help them identify what these feelings are by identifying *our* feelings. Children model themselves after adults, and our words "I feel sad that our cat died" indicate that it's okay for children to say how they feel, too.

God gives us emotions and expects us to use them. To suppress them in children with comments such as "Big boys don't cry" indicates that this part of God's creation should be suppressed. Rather, we should help children deal with emotions with God's help. He wants to help us and even invites us, in faith, to ask for that help.

Beverly Beckmann

Beverly Beckmann